Affirmation
Handwriting Workbook

Practice Handwriting Pages for Kids

Aa Bb Cc

Dear Parents, Guardians and Teachers,

Use this book to help the children in your life practice their handwriting skills.

Help them practice and internalize these positive affirmations daily (even when not using the book).

Some children may need your help making meaning of the affirmation sentences. Use these affirmations to remind them of how special they are.

This book belongs to:

Trace the Letters

A B C D E

F G H I J K

L M N O P

Q R S T U

V W X Y Z

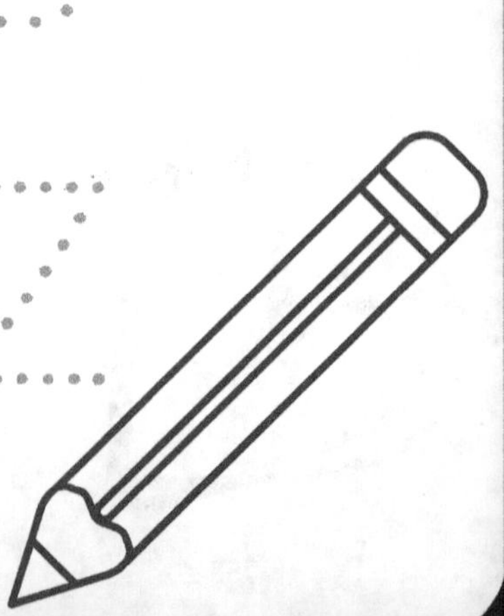

Trace the Letters

a b c d e

f g h i j k

l m n o p

q r s t u

v w x y z

# Trace the Letters

A B C D E

F G H I J K

L M N O P

Q R S T U

V W X Y Z

Trace the Letters

a b c d e

f g h i j k

l m n o p

q r s t u

v w x y z

I can do it.

I can do it.

I can do it.

I can do it.

I can do it.

I can do it.

Your turn

Write the affirmation sentence below.

I am worthy.

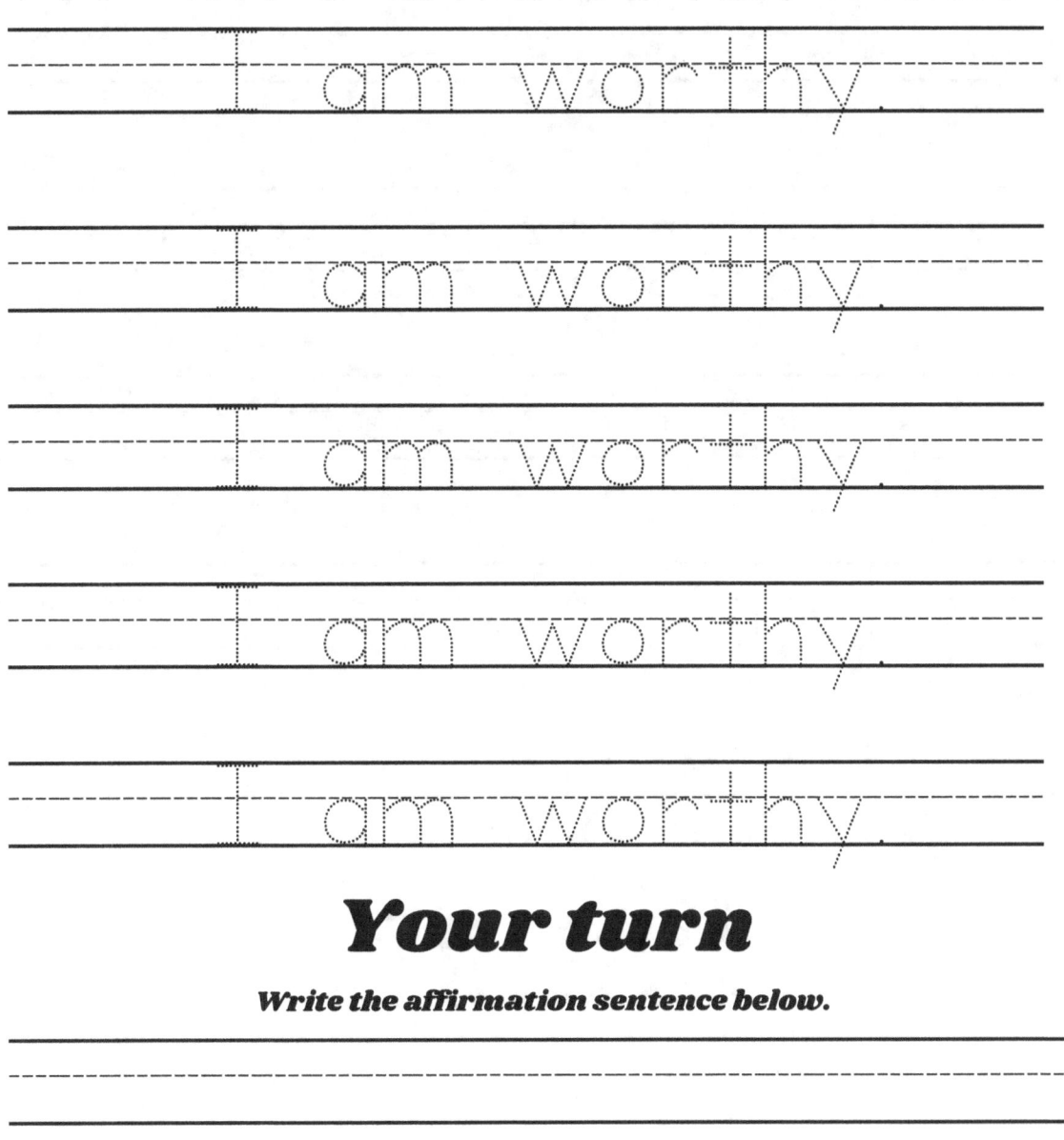

I am worthy.

I am worthy.

I am worthy.

I am worthy.

I am worthy.

Your turn

Write the affirmation sentence below.

My character matters.

My character matters.

My character matters.

My character matters.

My character matters.

My character matters.

Your turn

Write the affirmation sentence below.

I am caring.

I am caring.

I am caring.

I am caring.

I am caring.

I am caring.

Your turn

Write the affirmation sentence below.

I believe in myself.

I believe in myself.

I believe in myself.

I believe in myself.

I believe in myself.

I believe in myself.

Your turn

Write the affirmation sentence below.

believe →

I am grateful.

I am grateful.

I am grateful.

I am grateful.

I am grateful.

I am grateful.

Your turn

Write the affirmation sentence below.

I am proud of myself.

I am proud of myself.

I am proud of myself.

I am proud of myself.

I am proud of myself.

I am proud of myself.

Your turn

Write the affirmation sentence below.

I am enough.

I am enough.

I am enough.

I am enough.

I am enough.

I am enough.

Your turn

Write the affirmation sentence below.

My future is bright.

My future is bright.

My future is bright.

My future is bright.

My future is bright.

My future is bright.

Your turn

Write the affirmation sentence below.

I am focused.

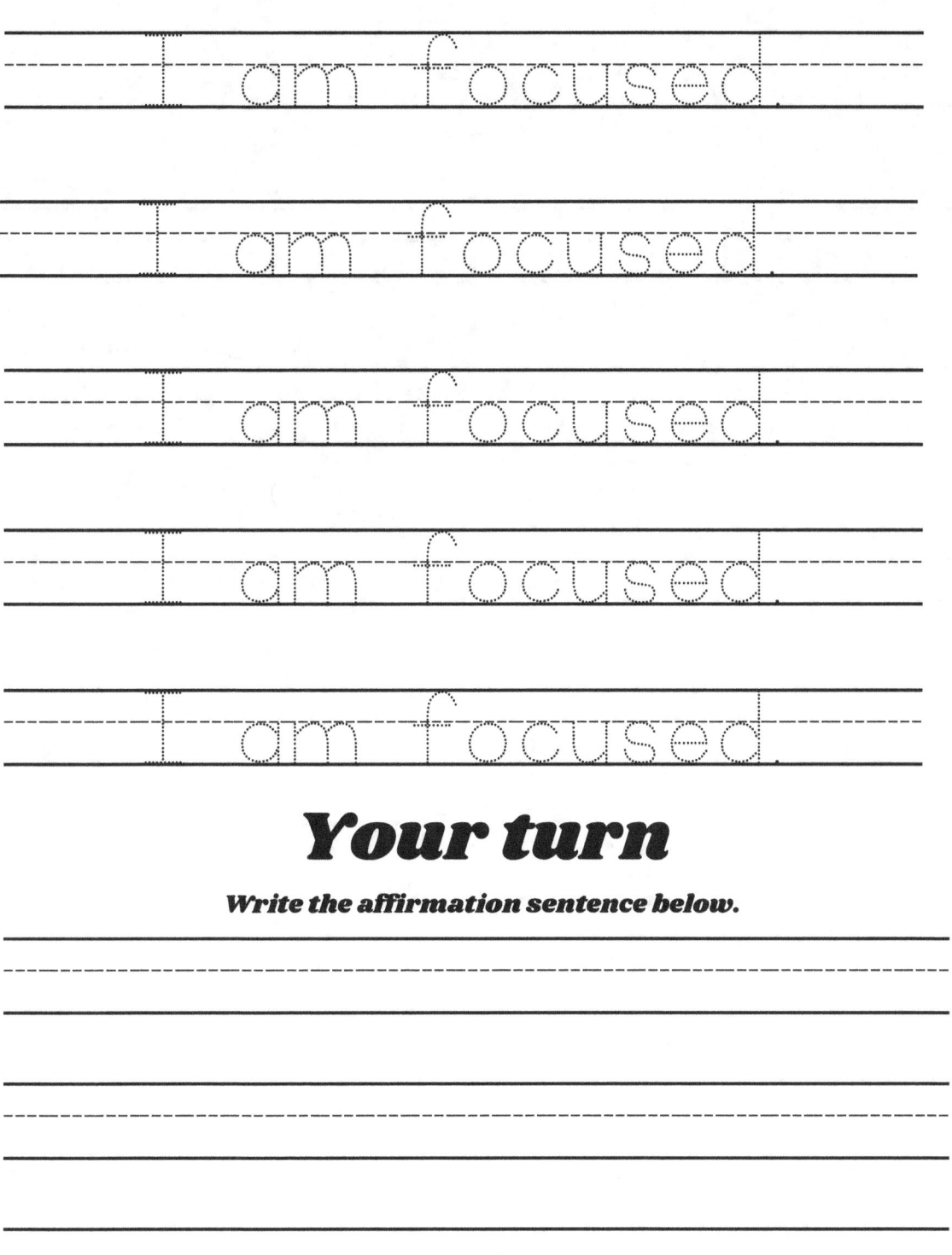

I am focused.

I am focused.

I am focused.

I am focused.

I am focused.

Your turn

Write the affirmation sentence below.

My voice matters.

My voice matters.

My voice matters.

My voice matters.

My voice matters.

My voice matters.

Your turn

Write the affirmation sentence below.

I am honest.

I am honest.

I am honest.

I am honest.

I am honest.

I am honest.

Your turn

Write the affirmation sentence below.

Mistakes help me grow.

Mistakes help me grow.

Mistakes help me grow.

Mistakes help me grow.

Mistakes help me grow.

Mistakes help me grow.

Your turn

Write the affirmation sentence below.

I am smart.

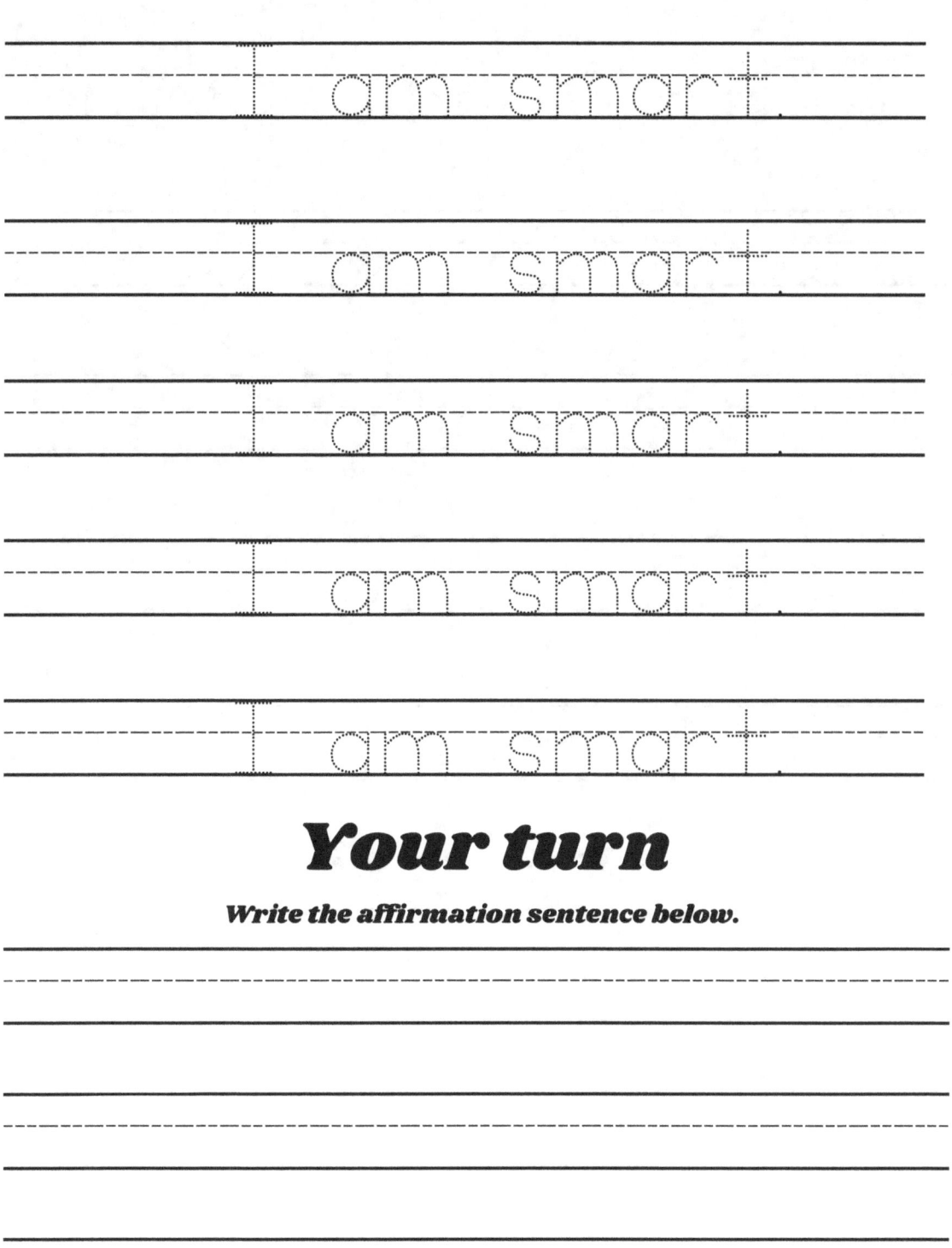

I am smart.

I am smart.

I am smart.

I am smart.

I am smart.

Your turn

Write the affirmation sentence below.

I have many talents.

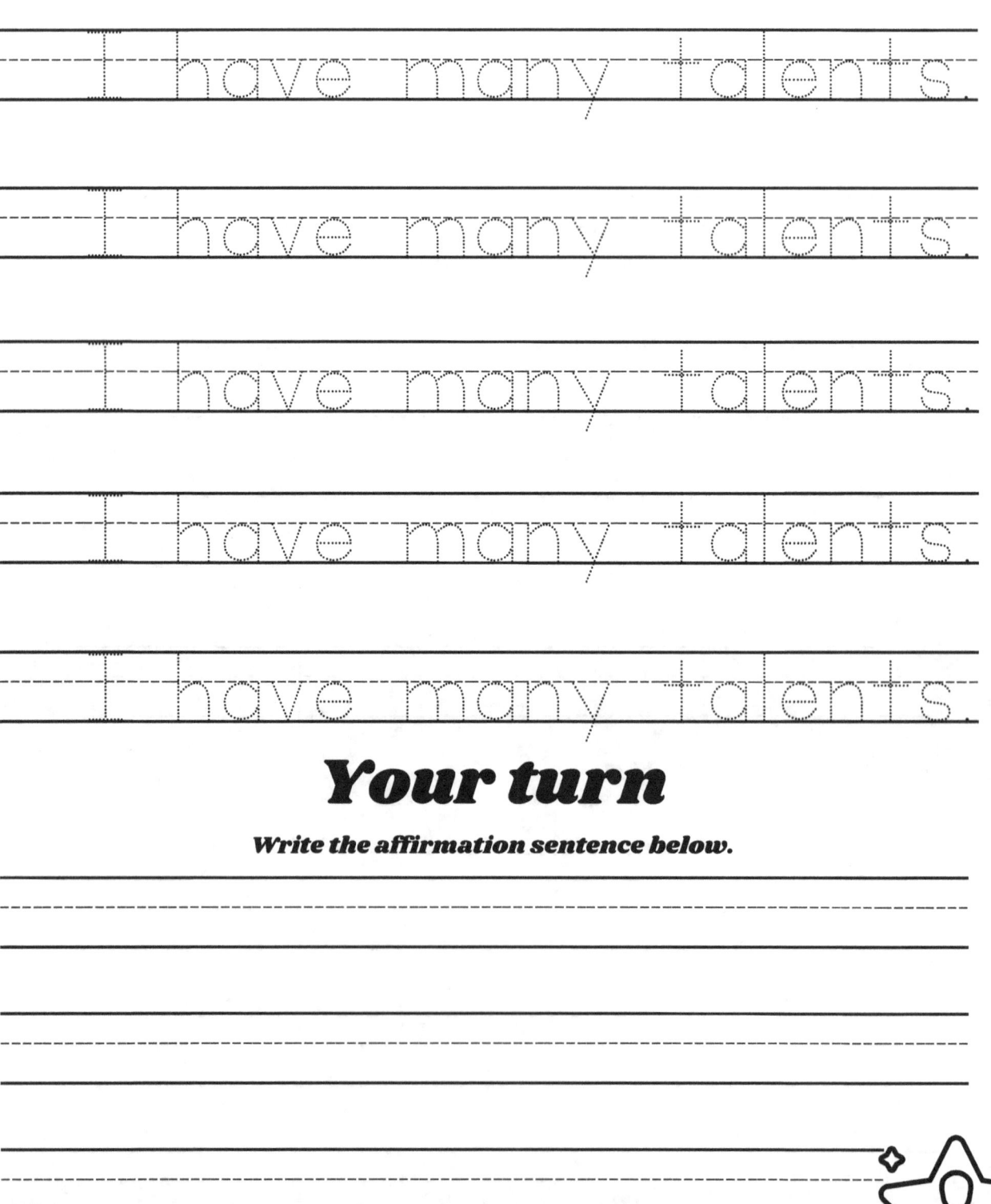

I have many talents.
I have many talents.
I have many talents.
I have many talents.
I have many talents.

Your turn

Write the affirmation sentence below.

I am special.

I am special.

I am special.

I am special.

I am special.

I am special.

Your turn

Write the affirmation sentence below.

I get better every day.

I get better every day.

I get better every day.

I get better every day.

I get better every day.

I get better every day.

Your turn

Write the affirmation sentence below.

I am kind.

I am kind.

I am kind.

I am kind.

I am kind.

I am kind.

Your turn

Write the affirmation sentence below.

I can always try again.

I can always try again.

I can always try again.

I can always try again.

I can always try again.

I can always try again.

Your turn

Write the affirmation sentence below.

I am determined.

I am determined.

I am determined.

I am determined.

I am determined.

I am determined.

Your turn

Write the affirmation sentence below.

I will be my best self.

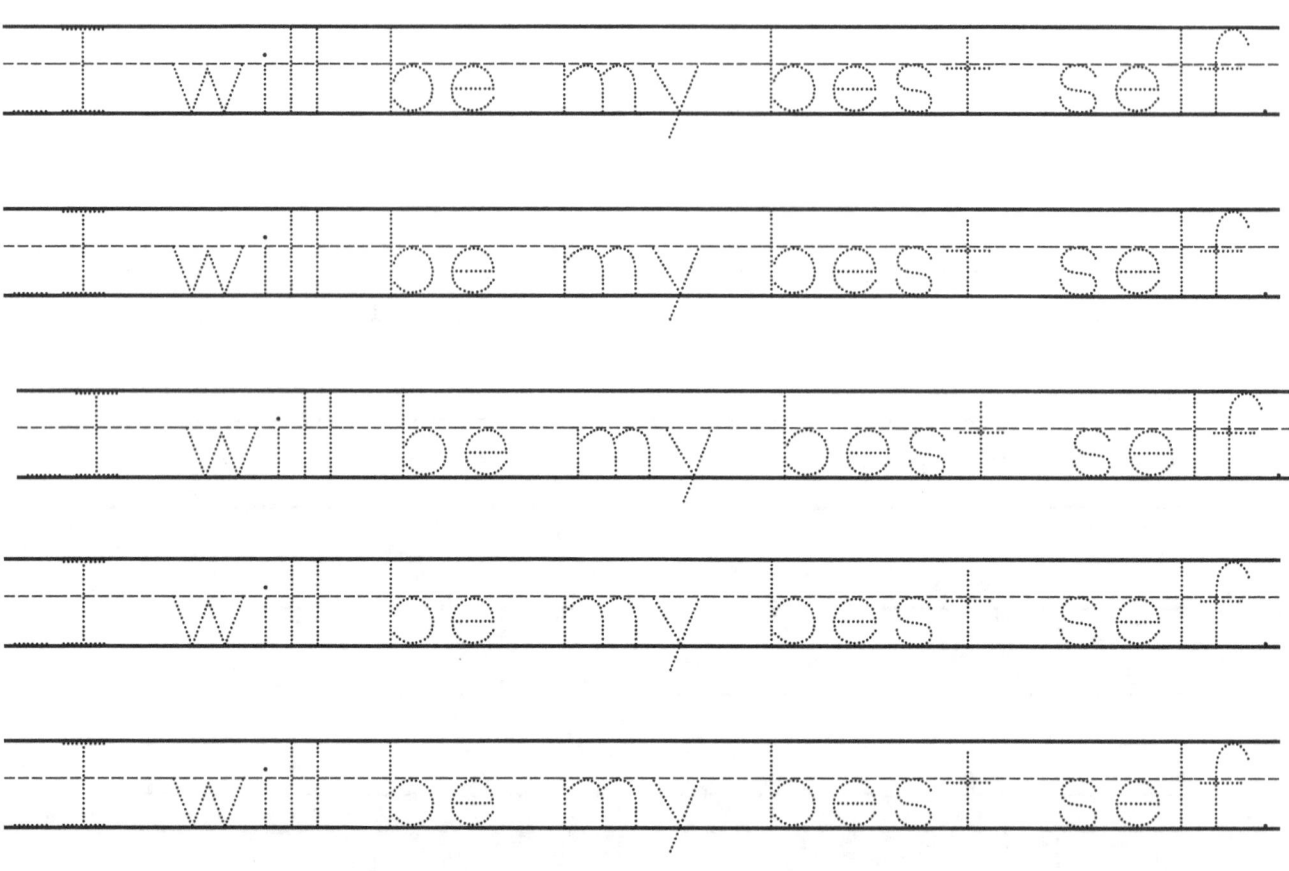

I will be my best self.

I will be my best self.

I will be my best self.

I will be my best self.

Your turn

Write the affirmation sentence below.

I am thankful.

I am thankful.
I am thankful.
I am thankful.
I am thankful.
I am thankful.

Your turn

Write the affirmation sentence below.

Each day is a new start.

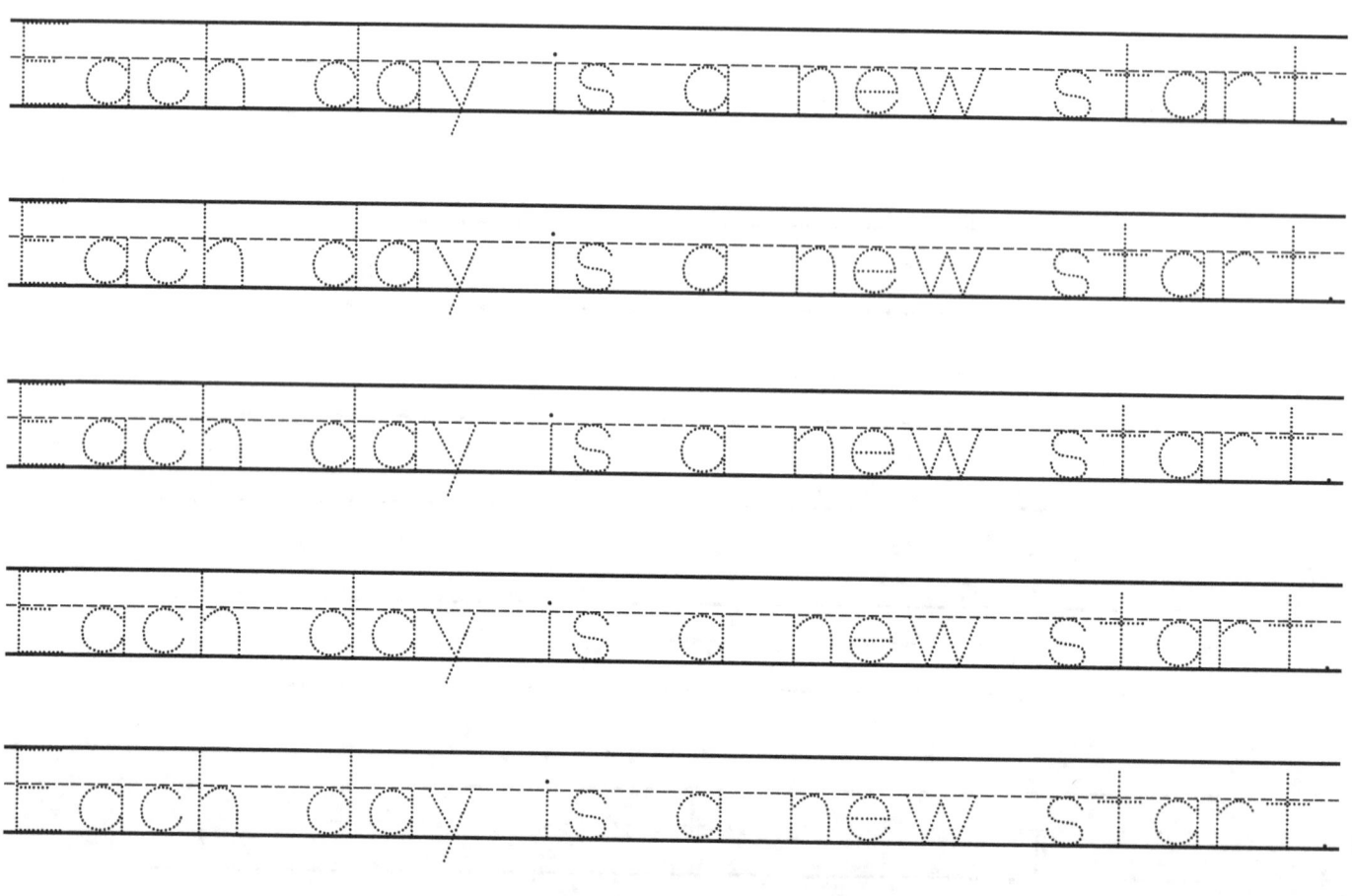

Each day is a new start.

Each day is a new start.

Each day is a new start.

Each day is a new start.

Each day is a new start.

Your turn

Write the affirmation sentence below.

START

I am loved.

I am loved.

I am loved.

I am loved.

I am loved.

I am loved.

Your turn

Write the affirmation sentence below.

I deserve to be happy.

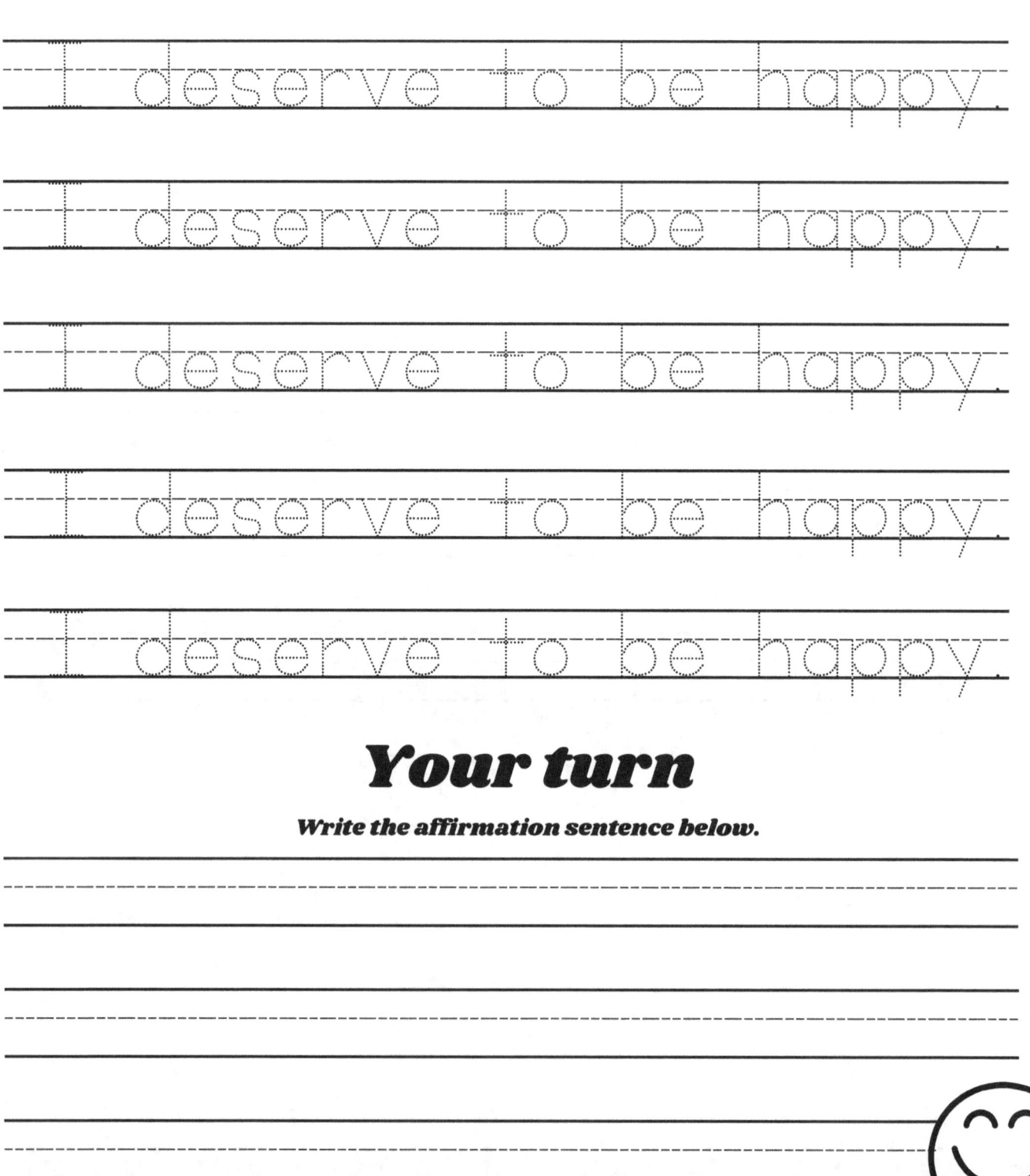

I deserve to be happy.

I deserve to be happy.

I deserve to be happy.

I deserve to be happy.

I deserve to be happy.

Your turn

Write the affirmation sentence below.

I am valued.

I am valued.

I am valued.

I am valued.

I am valued.

I am valued.

Your turn

Write the affirmation sentence below.

I try my hardest.

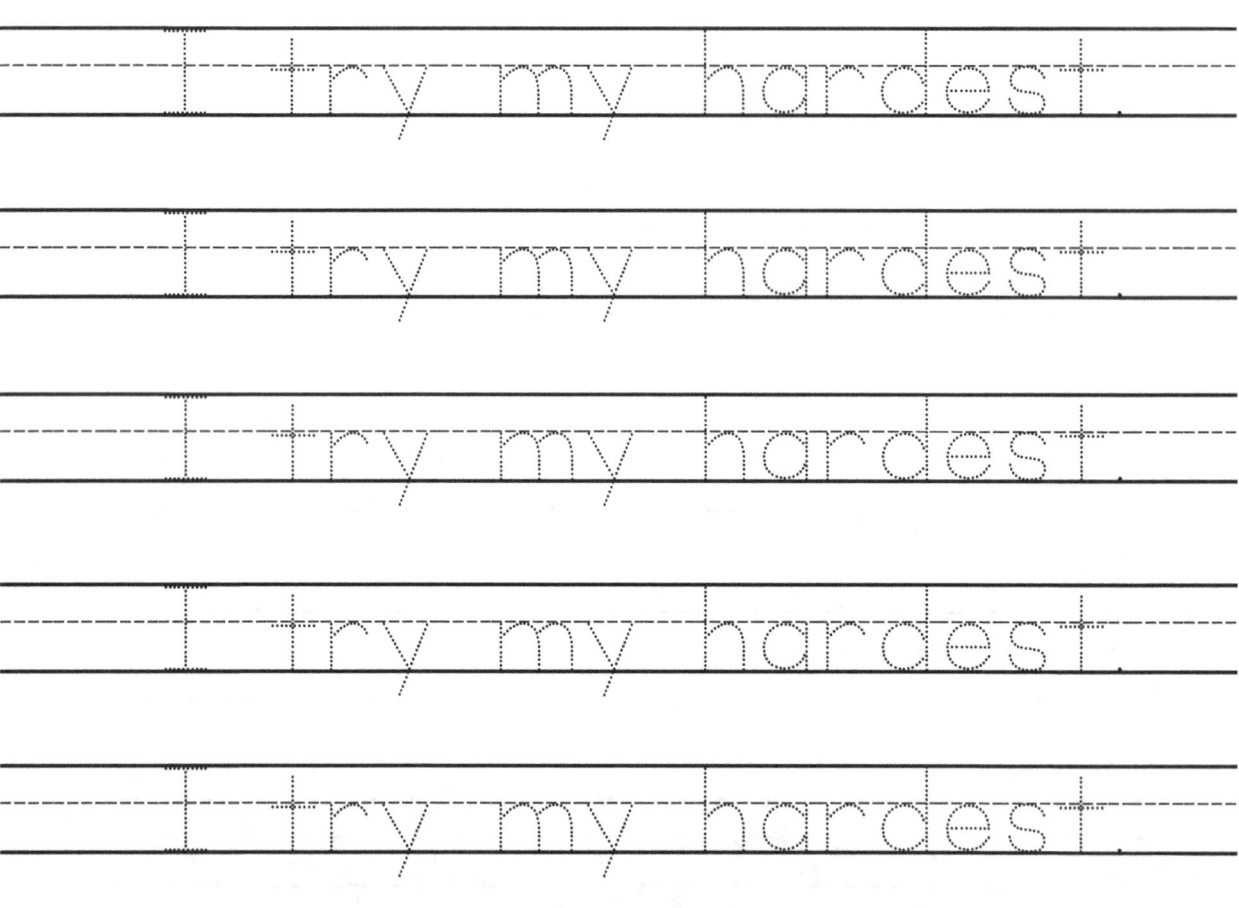

I try my hardest.
I try my hardest.
I try my hardest.
I try my hardest.
I try my hardest.

Your turn

Write the affirmation sentence below.

I am unique.

I am unique.

I am unique.

I am unique.

I am unique.

I am unique.

Your turn

Write the affirmation sentence below.

I can make a difference.

I can make a difference.

I can make a difference.

I can make a difference.

I can make a difference.

I can make a difference.

Your turn

Write the affirmation sentence below.

I am important.

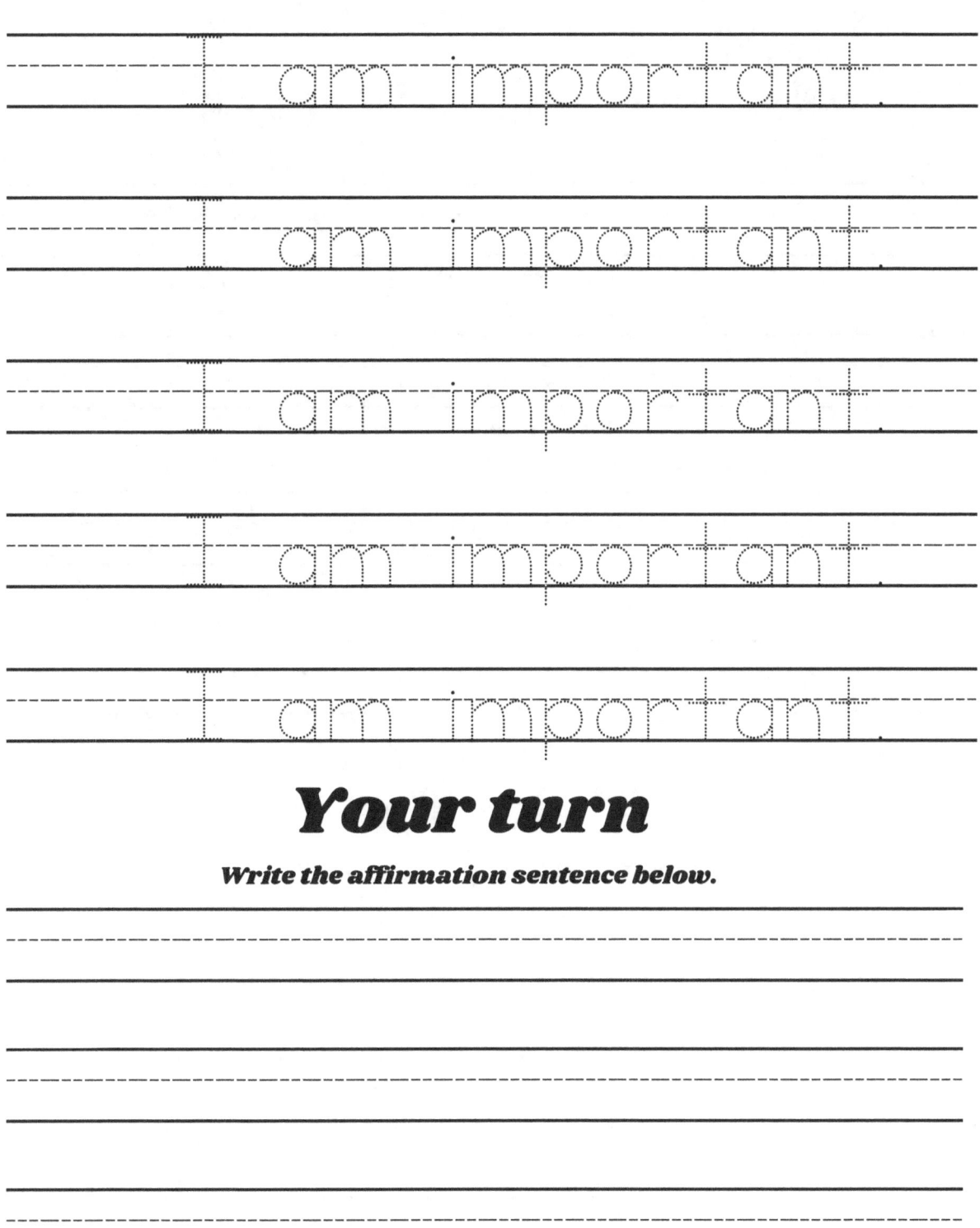

I am important.

I am important.

I am important.

I am important.

I am important.

Your turn

Write the affirmation sentence below.

I will try new things.

I will try new things.

I will try new things.

I will try new things.

I will try new things.

I will try new things.

Your turn

Write the affirmation sentence below.

I am responsible.

I am responsible.

I am responsible.

I am responsible.

I am responsible.

I am responsible.

Your turn

Write the affirmation sentence below.

I have important ideas.

I have important ideas.

I have important ideas.

I have important ideas.

I have important ideas.

I have important ideas.

Your turn

Write the affirmation sentence below.

IDEA

I am amazing.

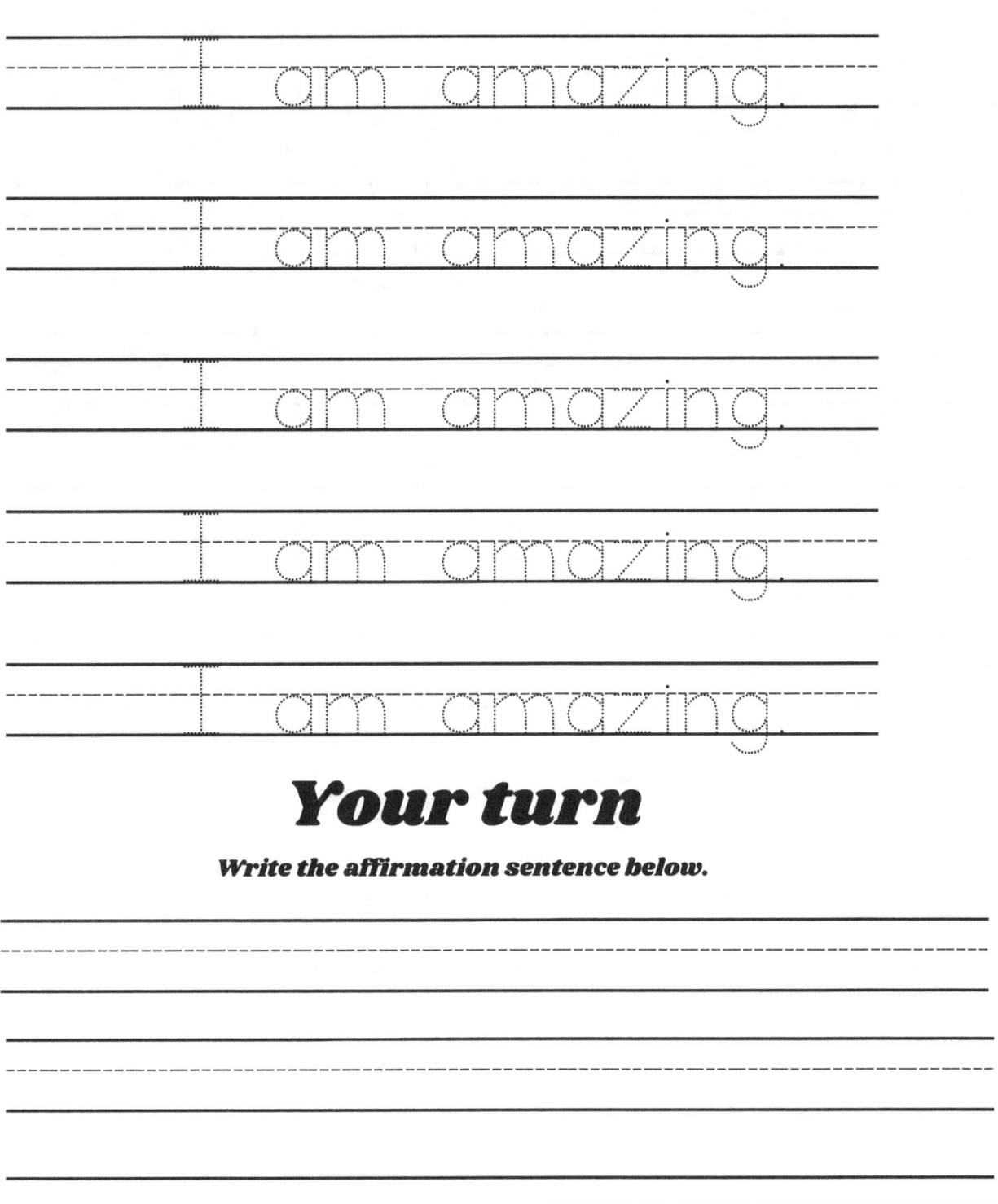

I am amazing.

I am amazing.

I am amazing.

I am amazing.

I am amazing.

Your turn

Write the affirmation sentence below.

I am one of a kind.

I am one of a kind.
I am one of a kind.
I am one of a kind.
I am one of a kind.
I am one of a kind.

Your turn

Write the affirmation sentence below.

I am respectful.

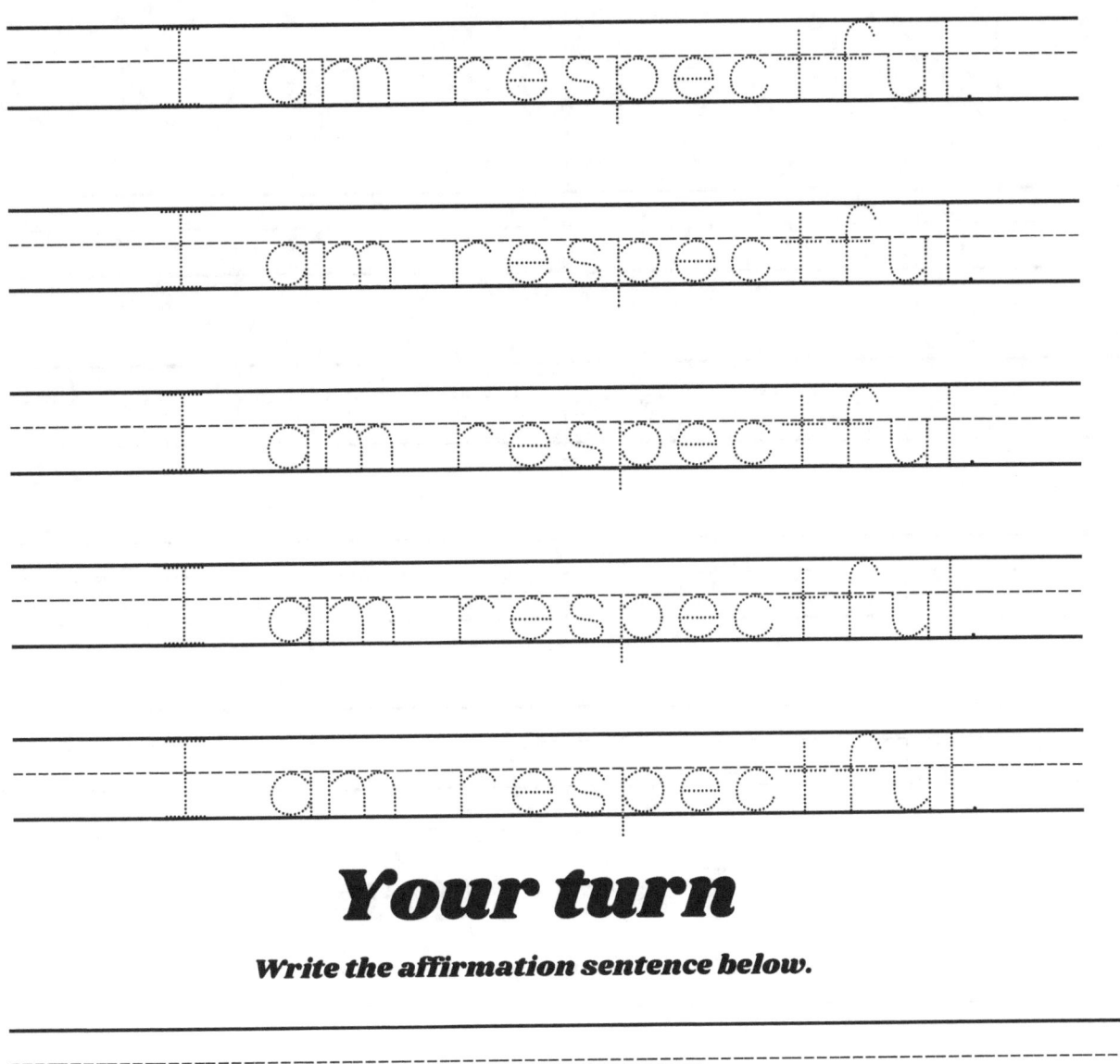

Your turn

Write the affirmation sentence below.

I have happy thoughts.

I have happy thoughts.

I have happy thoughts.

I have happy thoughts.

I have happy thoughts.

I have happy thoughts.

Your turn

Write the affirmation sentence below.

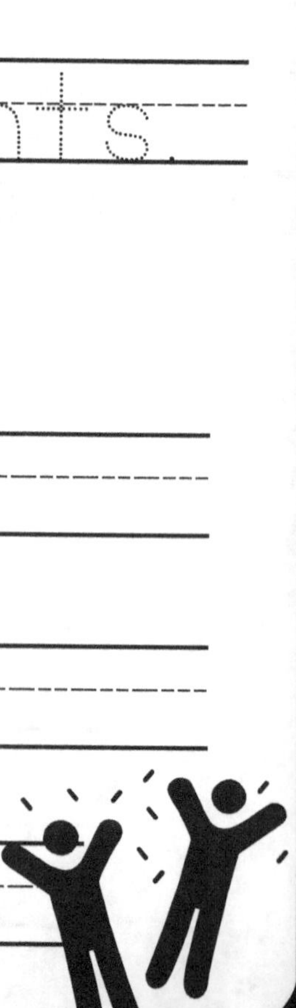

I am confident.

I am confident.

I am confident.

I am confident.

I am confident.

I am confident.

Your turn

Write the affirmation sentence below.

I am a good listener.

I am a good listener.

I am a good listener.

I am a good listener.

I am a good listener.

I am a good listener.

Your turn

Write the affirmation sentence below.

I am a good person.

I am a good person.

I am a good person.

I am a good person.

I am a good person.

I am a good person.

Your turn

Write the affirmation sentence below.

I am...

Trace the word. Write the word on the blank line.

powerful

happy

smart

amazing

loved

valued

caring

honest

special

I am...

Trace the word. Write the word on the blank line.

important

grateful

enough

kind

worthy

focused

thankful

confident

proud

Affirmations are short positive statements that you can repeat to practice self-love. Use these lines to write your own affirmations.

Affirmations are short positive statements that you can repeat to practice self-love. Use these lines to write your own affirmations.

_____

- -

_____

- -

_____

- -

_____

_____

- -

_____

_____

- -

_____

_____

- -

_____

_____

- -

_____

- -

_____

Affirmations are short positive statements that you can repeat to practice self-love. Use these lines to write your own affirmations.

Affirmations are short positive statements that you can repeat to practice self-love. Use these lines to write your own affirmations.

Write positive "I AM" affirmations below:

I am _____

I am _____

I am _____

I am _____

I am _____

I am _____

I am _____

I am _____

I am _____

I am _____

Write positive "I AM" affirmations below:

I am

I am

I am

I am

I am

I am

I am

I am

I am

I am

I am